Tea Ceremonies For Winter

Rolando Pérez

Coolgrove Press

Copyright © 2018 Rolando Pérez

Coolgrove Press, an imprint of
Cool Grove Publishing, Inc. New York.
512 Argyle Road, Brooklyn, NY 11218
All rights reserved under the International and
Pan-American Copyright Conventions.

www.coolgrove.com
For permissions and other inquiries write to info@coolgrove.com

ISBN 13: 978-1887276-89-4
ISBN 10: 1-887276-89-0
Library of Congress Control Number: 2018951537

Front cover art: The Tea Ceremony
by Kasamatsu Shirō (1954)

Back cover art: Two Bowls
by Severo Sarduy

Coolgrove Press is a past recipient of
Community of Literary Magazines and Presses **[CLMP]**'s
Face Out Re-grant funded by
the Jerome Foundation.

This book is distributed to the trade by **SPDBooks**

Media alchemy by Kiku

Coolgrove Press

*for my nephews Marlon and Sebastian
with love*

Other Coolgrove Press titles
by Rolando Pérez

The Divine Duty of Servants:
A Book of Worship
based on the artwork of Bruno Schulz (1999)

The Electric Comedy (2000)

The Lining of our Souls:
Excursions into selected paintings of
Edward Hopper (2002)

Tea Ceremonies for Winter

In winter silence is visible: the snow is silence become visible...Eternity is permeated by the great silence into which everything that has ever happened falls and disappears.

> Max Picard
> *The World of Silence*

White foods—white miso, bean curd, fish cake, the white meat of fish—lose much of their beauty in a bright room. A glistening black lacquer rice cask set off in a dark corner is both beautiful to behold and a powerful stimulus to the appetite... Our cooking depends upon shadows and is inseparable from darkness.

> Junichiro Tanizaki
> *In Praise of Shadows*

Born as we are out of chaos, why can we never establish contact with it? No sooner do we look at it than order, pattern, shape is born under our eyes. Never mind. Let it pass.

> Witold Gombrowicz
> *Cosmos*

Rolando Pérez

Tea Ceremonies for Winter

The other night on my way home a young man
sat next to me in the train, and immediately
placed his earphones on his head, turned on
I-phone and began to listen to music: so
loudly that I could hear every beat and every
word of the song he was listening to through
his headphones. This is a common occurrence
for anyone who rides the subway trains in
New York City. It is the way so many people
keep themselves from being engulfed
in the silence of meditation. Or what amounts
to the same thing, to being fully alive to the
world outside their seemingly protective noise.

SOME WORDS

It is said that what distinguishes words from iconic signs, is that words refer to things other than their material correlatives. That is to say, the word "white" not only refers to the quality of a thing; it also connotes...beyond our sensory perception of that color. In fact, *to mean* is just that: to transcend mere pictorial representation. Even the international STOP sign is more than iconic. The word STOP occurs inside a hexagon and the colors accompanying it are red (danger) and white (safety). This compulsion to ascribe meaning to the world is part of being human. One feels a sense of relief whenever one names a thing, because to establish ontology is to put the world in order. And order, even when we know is illusory, has always a calming effect upon the soul. Like the young man with the cell phone who drowns life in the loudness of music, we paint and write the *floating world:* because the *floating world* is what we fear.

  The Japanese tea ceremony is an attempt to impart meaning to that which would otherwise go unnoticed. After all, what is so different about serving, pouring, drinking tea, than the brushing of one's teeth? No-thing. What gives significance to the serving of the tea is the "ceremony" itself– or what in academic aesthetics is referred to as the *form*. For in the tea ceremony, the form *is* the content. A traditional haiku of the kind with which most people are familiar–the Bashō haiku–is almost always what we would call in the West, "banal". In comparison to the Western poem, "full of" meaning, allusions, mythologies, history, etc, a haiku may "just" describe a scene in nature: the landscape: a river, a tree, a bird, and not much else. But what the writer of the haiku always understood is that there is no such thing as just a landscape. Fortunately or unfortunately, the ego intercedes and fills in the scene with its own colors, sounds, smells, and "impressive" knowledge of literature.

Thus my goal in this humble volume was to be as faithful, insofar as that is possible—for a Westerner—to the spirit of the haiku. To let words stand in isolation, or in relation to other words, surrounded by the whiteness of the page, by the unsaid, free from the strictures of punctuation, free from the ever persistent ego, and free to the reader who is going to shape them and assign them his or her own meaning in any case. In short, what I wanted to achieve here--the relation between meaning and non-meaing, between sound and silence, between I and Not-I, constitutes a failed project—a project which (like jealousy) was doomed to fail from the very beginning. The attempt to express the inexpressible, to capture the ephemeral—everything that eludes us, and everything indeed eludes us--is what makes us human: our tragedy and our comedy, the spaces between darkness and light... as in the pages that follow...

Rolando Pérez

Tea Ceremonies for Winter

*Tea Ceremonies
(from the Momoyama Epoch)*

        Hot tea
        lacquer green
        cup
        smoke
        rising
        on a cold winter day.

White white hands
red red lips
precariously
sipping tea.

        Bamboo
        cup
        whispering
        softly
        naked
        like tea.

Rolando Pérez

Tea Ceremonies for Winter

```
Tea
 held
by
   a thin little string
and
    silence.
```

Tradition

```
Leaves in autumn
but red
green
no more.
```

```
          A tree
            branch
          heavy
          with snow

                 falls
            once
            again.
```

Rolando Pérez

One brick
then two
the camel
quietly expired
as smoke
from tea.

                    Stain
                    on napkin:
                    blood on snow
                no one has
                    seen
                        or
                    washed.

Night

Soft light
silent
songs
of crickets
that are not
there.

Tea Ceremonies for Winter

A solitary
    cloud
    covers
    the moon
    shines brighter.

At night
she hears
the bamboo
flute
and dreams
eternity.

Rolando Pérez

Tea Ceremonies for Winter

Morning

A saucer
a fork
a knife
slices
of
bread
in half.

      Two eggs
      sugar
      she
            steps on tiles:
      cold
            white feet
      pink toes.

Rolando Pérez

Feeling
the warm water
on her body
she thinks
of
the coming night.

                    Moist golden
                    crevice
                    the body
                    arches.

Brook

Water flows
down
a brook
slowly
in a dream
transparent blue.

Tea Ceremonies for Winter

Work

Time
urn
a bowl of rice
again
next
day.

Horseshoe
and nail
wounded
hands
galloping
to a river of salt.

Rolando Pérez

New York Skyline (Grey)
(December 12)

>Grey
>skyline
>yellow
>light
>in window
>a woman irons
>the eternal
>white
>sheet.

>On the 8th floor
>December day
>grey
>lost
>red Finch
>lights
>on a window sill.

Tea Ceremonies for Winter

Flight #101
    overhead
    flickering red
    wingtips disappear
    ashes
    inside a grey pocket.

    Water towers
    ice forming
    near
    distant
    peacefully
    untouched
    by others' eyes.

*New York Skyline #2
(December 19)*

>On the D train
>a bridge
>of blue scratchy patterns.

Out of the B
grey sky
grey waters
snow coming down
tugboats
dreaming.

>From a seat
>on the Q
>icicles
>hang
>from drainpipes
>outside
>the Chinese factory.

Rolando Pérez

Reading

At night
when everyone is gone
all the colors meet
present
and absent.

      Slowly
      under lamp
      or sun
      solitary eyes
      cross the bridge
      from left to right.

He lost his way
a character said
the beginning of Spring
did not return.

Tea Ceremonies for Winter

Anniversary

At one a.m.
at two a.m.
at three a.m.
they talk
late into the night
after
forty-one years.

Route 1, North

At fifty miles
per hour
snow
bare trees
gas stations
along the road.

Rolando Pérez

New Year's day
melancholy
snow
in New Jersey.

Betrayal

Unevenly
cut
    the taste of
    grapefruit.

Pillow
book
for another.

        Shirt's perfume
        bears
        paws in the snow.

Tea Ceremonies for Winter

Tundra
blood
voices of ghosts
echo.

Stan Getz (1927-1991)

Blue
smooth notes.
The sound of easy
cadent
sled.

Quarrel

The aftershocks
of silence
leave
a void
an avalanche
exhausted.

Rolando Pérez

Lawrenceville, N.J.

Like any other house
on the block
a car passes
with lights outside
in the winter
ice.

6 p.m.
burning wood
in the house
next door
with the kitchen light on.

Green sofa
yellow lamp
the floor above
writing
reading memories.

Tea Ceremonies for Winter

Rolando Pérez

Insomnia, 3:43 a.m.

   Rivers flowing
   beneath
   a whirlwind
   full of silence.

               Night
               without end
               turning
               and turning
               past
               possibilities.

Remembering
footfalls outside
a door
the termites eating wood.

Tea Ceremonies for Winter

The Future

Where once
horses neighed
one
by one
empty
house
remains.

"I crossed the bridge
with friends
when cherries blossomed
in Spring."

Rolando Pérez

*Fire Hydrant at St. John's Place, Brooklyn
(January 8, 1996)*

>Snuggled
>in snow
>naked
>to the touch.

Jealousy

>Eyes on
>hands
>lips
>a higher pitch
>different
>slight
>movements of wings
>inside.

Tea Ceremonies for Winter

Waiting
behind tree
with net
in hand
her butterfly
    lights on
    another flower.

        Secure
        loved
        in a cage
        she watches
        her hummingbird
        die
        forever.

Rolando Pérez

Rum on the rocks (music)

Dark
rum
yellowish
with afternoon
sunlight
dissolving.

        Ice cubes
        chime
        touching
        side of glass.

Between
small
sharp
cracks of ice
silence (   )
in water
music.

Rain

Running
in the rain
wind
bends
the skeleton
of an umbrella.

Lying in bed
face up
the rain
tick-tocks
on tin roof
years ago
on an island.

Rolando Pérez

A dream (in Jamaica)

Imposing: black
flat with windows
high-rise
ship
sails
on a dark bay
night
running
over
two small boats
there again
after passing.

Exhaustion
Day comes
early
to labor
the dream
of soft pillows.

Tea Ceremonies for Winter

The bow
aches
its strings
pulled
too many times.

        Quiet
        at work
        dying
        light
        of another
        grey day.

Out of breath
on a leash
walked
by boy
dog no longer
barked.

Rolando Pérez

Television

Three colors
one light
illumines
all
in every
house
screaming monkeys.

Nico (After a movie)

Beautifully
wrapped
heavy
in darkness
she went
opening doors
releasing us
to little deaths
without gods.

Tea Ceremonies for Winter

Elegance (and Being)

>Always white
>bare
>flimsy
>the essential
>paper lantern
>pausing
>with shadows.

>>Red shirt
>>eyes
>>of blue
>>folded
>>arms
>>and a fall
>>in April
>>of height and hair
>>at a conference of birds.

Tea Ceremonies for Winter

Pretty feet

Small
delicate
toes
with red
nail
polish
thinking
of Tanizaki
travelling
west.

Wine
    Red
    becoming
    sleepy
        softly
        glassy
        on your breasts.

Rolando Pérez

Saké

Drinking saké
a hand follows
the contours of your back
warmly
    slowly
        down:
your mouth
like rice.

Ending

In a dark room
a candle flame
between
two fingers
pressed
then out.

Tea Ceremonies for Winter

Meow Meow Meow

A cat
she
knows how
to fall
without getting hurt.

Somei Sato (b. 1947)

Children's
little steps
toward
midnight
lacquer
lining
our souls
with music.

Rolando Pérez

Staten Island Ferry

Cold night
snow
falling
on water
looking out
the ferry's window
on the way
to visit a friend.

*Portrait of old woman at 100
(Ruika)*
    Wrinkled
    knotted
    hands
    lost
    that time
    when she cooked
    she was
    everything.

Tea Ceremonies for Winter

Rolando Pérez

When she was
November
came
and the earth
reclaimed
without a whisper
a century of
furrows.

Miso soup (Miró's colours)

How beautiful it is
the beige in black
bowl
decorated with seaweed
green.

Tea Ceremonies for Winter

Friends
> In an empty room
> she lit a candle
> two
> when it was dark.

Love
> Fragile
> bowl of tea
> shared delicately
> at chanoyu.
>
> After tea ceremony
> he thinks of his guests
> walking home
> together.

Rolando Pérez

Tea Ceremonies for Winter

Ancient bowls
side by side
on table
next to kettle
warm
speak, say.

"Tea ceremonies for winter"

> Brief
> instants
> the potential
> fullness
> of zero.

                A tall tree
                planted
                deep
                facing west
                bends
                to the wind.

Rolando Pérez

Tea Ceremonies for Winter

      Like paper
           blown by wind
      important
      and not
      without
      destination.

Color-less
taste-less
water
a shadow
between my fingers
fails.

Rolando Pérez

Tea Ceremonies for Winter

Afterword

I wrote *Tea Ceremonies for Winter* more than twenty years ago, just a year or two before *The Divine Duty of Servants* (1999), a book based on the drawings of Bruno Schulz depicting scenes of masochism and foot fetishism. And in the preface I wrote:

> If the question of matter or the materiality of existence was central in his [Schulz's] fiction...it was also to be found in his drawings of masochism and foot fetishism— for nothing is closer to the materiality of existence, to the earth, if you will, than humility and foot fetishism. To be humiliated is to be lowered, to be brought down to the earth (*humus*), to have one's spirit returned to the earth. And what part of our body is closer to the earth than our feet?

On the face of it, *Tea Ceremonies for Winter* and *The Divine Duty of Servants* seem to be very different books, sharing absolutely no qualities. But that is only because we are used to looking at the world in atomistic ways, where actual entities are thought to be singular and distinct from all others. In other words, because we live in a capitalist epoch, we tend to emphasize the "private" life of objects ("windowless monads" in Leibnizian terms) instead of their "public" lives;—that is to say, we fail to understand that objects are relational. And because that is the case, an object is nothing more and nothing less than the reality of an event. Think of an atom with its nucleus made up of protons and neutrons, and they in turn, made up of quarks. An atom is always an event in a nest of some kind (or molecule). What then, connects the "molecule" of Schulz's aesthetic foot fetishism in *The Divine Duty of Servants* to the "molecule" of the free-form "haikus" of *Tea Ceremonies for Winter*? The answer is quite simple: nature, the earth. After all, feet, trees, and snow, are ontologically not very different from each other.

Ever since I can remember, I have been fascinated with the supposedly "dead" or inanimate objects with which we share our lives—objects like pens, tooth brushes, hammers, etc.,—and our ontological relation to them, which has always seem to me much more profound and mysterious than we acknowledge. This internal relation is what fascinates me about the traditional Japanese haiku, and particularly that of a writer like Bashō who allows for non-human objects (of *natura naturans* or *poiseis*) to speak their being. To accomplish such a task, is quite difficult, especially for a Westerner. This is not an attack on Western culture, but rather a description. Cultures are very complex organisms, and by that token irreducible to one-dimensional descriptions. Having said that, however, one particularly negative trait of Western culture is its overvaluation of the ego, wherein the *I* through his or her "own" sense of self-importance ends up harming others (human and non-human), and ultimately him or herself.

Tea Ceremonies for Winter

What the Bashō haiku remarkably accomplishes is to bracket the imperial *I* of subjectivity in order that for one very brief moment (the duration of the poem), we humans conceive of ourselves as objects on an equal ontological plane with all the other entities. And so in the haiku, natural objects, despite its author's best intentions, are fetishized, in ways not very differently than the submissive fetishist of Schulz's drawings who fetishizes feet. I understand that since Marx the word "fetish" and its association with "commodity fetishism" is thought in negative terms; it is a way, we are told, of giving "transcendental," "mystical" qualities to inanimate objects (undeserving of such bestowals), and it is also putatively a way of "objectifying people," of turning humans into objects. But this too is a prejudice of our Anglo-Protestant culture and epoch that projects an image of thought congruent of a subject-object distinction, wherein the subject corresponds to the fullness of the soul and the object to the "empty vessel" that is the body. And we all know the great fear that Anglo-Protestant culture, generally feels towards the body. Nobody wants to be "treated" like an object, except when they are sick, then CAT scans, MRIs, and prescription medications, are all welcome.

There are cultures, however, that have a more expansive ontology, and as such, their cosmologies are inclusive rather than exclusive. Many African and Amerindian cultures are like this. What we know of them and of their cosmologies, obviously for most of us, come from the outside, just as haikus are in some ways external to us. However, anthropologists sensitive to perspectival differences have attempted to communicate their world-views and their ways of life. In *Cannibal Metaphysics*, for example, Brazilian anthropologist Eduardo Viveiros de Castro cites the now famous passage from Lévi-Strauss' *Tristes Tropiques* concerning Amerindian and European perspectives regarding the body and soul. Not long after the conquest of the "New World," the Spaniards sent out an expedition to one of the islands of the Greater Antilles, to investigate whether the "Indians" indeed had souls, reports Lévi-Strauss. The "Indians," for their part, drowned their European prisoners, and observed their cadavers over a long period of time, in order to find out if the bodies of the Europeans were subject to putrefaction. Viveiros de Castro interprets the event this way: "The Europeans never doubted that the Indians had bodies—animals have them too—whereas the Indians never doubted that the Europeans had souls, since animals and the ghosts of the dead do as well." What the Amerindians wanted to find out, according to Viveiros de Castro, was whether "the others' souls or spirits could possess a body materially similar to theirs"—no doubt puzzled by the Europeans' use of torture in the colonies. One of the most exciting and controversial anthropologists writing today, Viveiros de Castro, has been instrumental in giving voice to the ontological perspective of the Amazonian Araweté, for whom the human/non-human (animal) distinction is articulated differently than in the West. Amazonians, says Viveiros de Castro, do not differentiate between humans and animals the way we do. Interestingly, for them "[t]he original common condition of both humans and animals is not animality, but rather humanity." This, without a doubt, constitutes a reversal of the Darwinian concept of evolution.

And in Lydia Cabrera's *Cuentos negros de Cuba/Afro-Cuban Tales*, the author gives us a glimpse into the kind of ontological perspectives that were communicated by Afro-Cubans in the form of oral tales. In Cabrera's retelling of the tales, one encounters, as with the Amerindian myths, animals that possess human qualities (e.g., "Bregantino Bregantín," "Papa Turtle, Papa Tiger"), and even the hair of a beautiful African woman that becomes indistinguishable from the of undulating currents of a river and its green-colored silt ("The Green Mud of the Almendares"). Most of the tales that Cabrera compiled over the years were of Yoruba origins. As is well known by now, what goes by the name of "santería"—the syncretic religion of many Caribbean countries—emerged from the Yoruba religion of African slaves brought to the "New World." The Santería rituals that invoke the name of deities or orishas like Changó, Yemayá, and Obatalá, involve the use of living and non-living objects, from chickens to leaves to sea shells; in other words, the employment of fetish objects.

Remarkably, the Spanish philosopher, José Ortega y Gasset, argued as far back as 1915 against the subject-object binary that has for a long time set humans atop an ontological hierarchy, relegating non-human and inanimate objects to the status of servile entities whose sole purpose is to satisfy us. In "An Essay in Esthetics by Way of a Preface" Ortega wrote:

> There is the same difference between a pain that someone tells me about and a pain that I feel as there is between the red that I see and the being red of...[a] red leather box. *Being red* is for it what hurting is for me. Just as there is an I-John Doe, there is also an I-red, an I-water, and an I-star. Everything, from a point of view within itself, is an "I."

Ortega here anticipated what Viveiros de Castro has referred to as the cosmological perspectivism of Amerindians. And Ortega also here expressed what many non-Western cultures have felt for millennia: that we live in a complicit ontological and even existential relationship with all objects in the universe, living and non-living. But now a word of caution: the question should never revolve around the infantile, competitive issues of origin and precedence. The deep well of Western philosophy is inexhaustible, and I will not join the chorus of those who, given the opportunity, would reduce it to a stereotype, the product of their reductive ignorance. The universe is thick and wide; one supernova does not a ripple make. North, south, east, and west are not the names of territories, but rather of highly complex events that relate to each other through vectors. As philosopher and mathematician, Alfred North Whitehead wrote in *Process and Reality:* "A traveler, who has lost his way, should not ask, Where am I? What he really wants to know is, Where are the other places?"

Today, nearly one hundred years after Ortega and Whitehead, some Western philosophers like Graham Harman—there are not many—have returned to the question of beings. This is what Harman's *oject-oriented-ontology* is all about—replacing the old hierarchical ontology of subjects and objects with a flat and democratic ontology that envisions such things as nails, printers, and notebooks as possessing a depth that is as inaccessible to us as that of humans, and even our own. Now, as abstract as all this may sound, with its hints of pre-modern animism, nothing in fact, could be more concrete. The plain fact is that we are destroying the planet: most of the world's oceans, lakes, rivers, and streams are contaminated with carcinogenic pollutants; there are entire sections of the Pacific Ocean that are covered with plastic for thousands of miles; the soil is being destroyed through the exploitation of fossil fuels and fracking; in many cities of the world the air is literally un-breathable without the use of masks due to the greenhouse gas emissions emanating from chemical plants and automobiles, and water as a privatized entity is becoming a commodity, instead of something that we can all equally enjoy. Nothing else explains this ontological turn in Western philosophy, than our destruction of nature and the bleak direction in which we are headed. Geologists have called our age of global warming, the "Anthropocene"—the epoch that corresponds to the human manipulation, domination, and destruction of the earth's ecosystem. This is, in part, what I feared and wrote about in *The Electric Comedy* (2000). Now it seems to me that if we continue to treat non-human objects like mountains, rivers, oceans, the air, the animals of the earth, as mere things for-us, and fail to respect these objects both ontologically and existentially, we will not only destroy them, but destroy ourselves in a very short period of time, as we are all part of the same organism. To avoid that we need to acknowledge with Ortega, Jane Bennett (below), and many non-Western cultures, that the *I-ness*, the internal life of objects, summons an ethical response from us. In her brilliant book, *Vibrant Matter: A Political Ecology of Things*, Jane Bennett puts it this way:

> The discourse of environmentalism has certainly raised good political questions...Yet other questions have been occluded: How can humans become more attentive to the public activities, affects, and effects of non-humans? What dangers do we risk if we continue to overlook the force of things? What other affinities between us and them become apparent if we construe both us and them as *vibrant matter*? (my italics)

Significantly, Bruno Schulz also saw it this way. For the Polish writer all matter pulsated with life. In *Cinnamon Shops* (also translated as *The Street of Crocodiles*), the narrator's "father", who worships his servant, Adela's feet, pointedly declares:

> "The Demiurge....had no monopoly on creation; creation is a privilege of all spirits. Matter has been granted infinite fecundity, an inexhaustible vital force, and at the same time, a seductive power of temptation that entices us to create forms. In the depths of matter, indistinct smiles take shape, tensions are reinforced, experimental shapes solidify. All matter flows from the infinite possibilities passing through it in faint shivers..." There was no end to my father's glorification of the bizarre element that is matter. "There is no dead matter," he instructed us; "lifelessness is only an external appearance behind which unknown forms of life are hiding."

No greater poetic statement has ever been made concerning the vitalitsm of matter--at least that I know of in Western literature—than this. But perhaps its major fault lies in the fact that the Father's materialism, which informs his fetishism, is still too connected to a subjectivity that sees the vibrant material object as an object *made* by the "Demiurge" specifically *for* him, for his pleasure. At the end of the Father's disquisition on the life of matter and of mannequins in particular, we are told, Adela "slid forward a few inches with her chair, lifted the hem of her dress, slowly extended her foot in its tight fitting black silk, and flexed it like a serpent's head" for him. Such a scene has no place, however, in a haiku, with its depictions of nature, which aims as much as possible to extract subjectivity from the landscape. This is not to say that sensuality is absent from the haiku, not at all. It just takes a different form.

Rolando Pérez

Take for example the following three haikus by Bashō:

> As they begin to rise again
> Chrysanthemums faintly smell
> After the flooding rain.
>
> bush—clover flowers—
> they sway but do not drop
> their beads of dew.
>
> an ancient pond
> a frog jumps in
> the splash of water.

Here nature is presented in a very different way than in the Romantic tradition. The objects of nature simply *are*—they exist for themselves. If they are "sublime," they are not so for us; "sublime" is the way we interpret their inaccessibility, and everything that they "withhold" from us. One poet, a Zen master himself, who has given expression to such a view of nature, is none other than the American poet, Gary Snyder--lately, the subject of *Mountains, Rivers, And the Great Earth: Reading Gary Snyder and Dōgen* by Jason M. Wirth, a philosopher who synthesizes in creative ways the Eastern and the Western philosophical and literary traditions. Consequently, on the very notion of the ontological and existential depth of all objects—that we have been discussing—Snyder had this to say in *The Real Work: Interviews and Talks, 1964-1979*:

> ...I have had a very moving, profound perception a few times that everything was alive (the basic perception of animism) and that on one level there is no hierarchy of qualities in life—that the life of a stone or a weed is as completely beautiful and

authentic, wise and valuable as the life of, say, an Einstein. And that Einstein and the weed know this…

Our failure to recognize this, to endorse a flat ontology, what Levi R. Bryant, has called a "democracy of objects," will inevitably lead to the destruction of the planet. The great Aldo Leopold long ago called for an ethics that would include the protection of non-human objects. And Graham Harman in *Dante's Broken Hammer* argues for an object-oriented ontology that is the union of ethics and aesthetics. Harman's exemplar is Dante, but it could equally be Bashō and the tradition of the haiku, to which I have tried my best to pay homage in this humble, little book that is *Tea Ceremonies for Winter*—an invitation to multiple (prosaic and profound) events—an offering and a cup of tea. "There is nothing in the real world which is merely an inert fact," wrote Whitehead in *Process and Reality*. "Every reality is there for feeling [physical and conceptual]; it promotes feeling, and it is felt. Also there is nothing which belongs merely to the privacy of feeling of one individual actuality." That is because the energy communicated between things is what he calls "feelings." And feelings, insofar as they are shared--and they are always shared, even if silently as it happens with autistic individuals and atoms—occur in a nexus.

> Ancient bowls
> side by side
> on table
> next to kettle
> warm
> speak, say.

Rolando Pérez

Yes, indeed "we are all in this together"—but that "we" also includes mountains, rivers, paper bags, plants, rocks, tea leaves, light bulbs, combs, hammers, mice, etc. This shared energy—between subatomic particles, plants and butterflies, people and tea cups—is what some philosophers have called "love." And "love," as Leonard Cohen sings in *The Future*, "is the only engine of survival."

Bibliography

Bashō, Matsuo. *Bashō's Haiku: Selected Poem of Matsuo Bashō.* Translation and introduction by David Landis Barnhil. Albany: SUNY Press, 2004.

Bennett, Jane. *Vibrant Matter: A Political Ecology of Things.* Durham: Duke University Press, 2010.

Bryant, Levi R. *The Democracy of Objects.* Ann Arbor: Open Humanities Press, 2011.

Cabrera, Lydia. *Afro-Cuban Tales.* Translated by Alberto Hernández-Chiroldes and Lauren Yoder. Introduction by Isabel Castellanos. Lincoln: University of Nebraska Press, 2004.

Harman, Graham. *Dante's Broken Hammer: The Ethics, Aesthetics, and Metaphysics of Love.* London: Repeater Books, 2016.

Ortega y Gasset, José. "An Essay in Esthetics by Way of a Preface." *Phenomenology and Art.* Trans. Philip W. Silver. New York: W.W. Norton, 1975.

Schulz, Bruno. *Collected Stories.* Translated by Madeline G. Levine. Foreword by Rivka Galchen. Evanston: Northwestern University Press, 2018.

Snyder, Gary. *The Real Work: Interviews and Talks, 1964-1979.* Edited by William Scott McLean. New York: New Directions, 1980.

Viveiros de Castro, Eduardo. *Cannibal Metaphysics.* Translated and edited by Peter Skafish. Minneapolis: Univocal, 2014.

Whitehead, Alfred North. *Process and Reality.* Corrected Edition. Eds. David Ray Griffin and Donald S. Sheburne. New York: The Free Press, 1985.

Wirth, Jason M. *Mountains, Rivers, and the Great Earth: Reading Gary Snyder and Dōgen.* Albany: SUNY Press, 2017.

Tea Ceremonies for Winter

Image Credits

The Tea Ceremony (1954; front cover, p. 6) is a woodblock print by Tokyo born artist, Kasamatsu Shirō (1898-1991). Kasamatsu Shirō developed the *shin-hanga* (new prints) style post his Shōzaburō Watanabe period, when he began to publish with Unsōdō Publishing in Kyoto in the early 1950s. This print is in the public domain.

Two Bowls (back cover, p. 4), date unknown, and *Les etangs de la Reine Blanche-Hiver* / The pool of the White Queen – Winter (1983; p. 46), are by Cuban writer and artist Severo Sarduy (1937-1993). Severo Sarduy is considered one of the most important Latin American writers of the twentieth century. *Two Bowls* and *Les etangs de la Reine Blanche - Hiver* (1983) are in the François Wahl Archives at Princeton University. Special thanks to the Department of Rare Books and Special Collection at the Princeton University Library, for allowing me to use these images. Sarduy's writing and pictorial work was highly influenced by Japanese aesthetics.

Solitary walker (2017; p. vi), and *Bare Light Trees* (2017; p. 52) is a photograph by Professor Nuria Morgado, who teaches contemporary Spanish literature at The College of Staten Island and The Graduate Center of the City University of New York. Special thanks to Nuria Morgado for allowing me to use her photographs.

Placid Sea Ferry (2018; p. 10) is a photo by Alisa Yalan; a photographer and graphic designer, and the mother of two inspiring daughters from China, Jade and Lia. Special thanks to Alisa for allowing me to use her photograph.

Before the Mirror (1916; p. 34) is by *shin-hanga* artist, Shinsui Itō (1898-1972). *Before the Mirror*, which depicts a woman in a deep red kimono that contrasts with her black hair and her white skin, was Itō's first major work. It was published by art publisher Shōzaburō Watanabe (1885-1962), the driving force behind the Japanese *shin-hanga*, printmaking movement. This print is in the public domain.

Meguro Drum Bridge and Sunset Hill (1857; p. 42) is by the famous Japanese artist of the Edo period, Utagawa Hiroshige (1797-1885). One of 118 sheets, *Meguro Drum Bridge* is from Hiroshige's series, *One Hundred Famous Views of Edo*, which he began to work on sometime around 1848, the last decade of his life. This print is in the public domain.

The remaining images in this book were photographs taken by the author:

" *Two Cups in Green*" (2018), p. iii

"*Little Bird*" (2018), p. 15.

Ice, After Snowfall (c. 1978), p. 23.

Foggy Bridge (2018), p. 39.

Winter Light: Tree (2018), p. 44.

Tea Ceremonies for Winter

About the author

Rolando Pérez is professor of Spanish and Latin American literature and philosophy in the Romance Languages Department of Hunter College—CUNY. He is the author of numerous publications on the Neo-Baroque, and the relation between literature, the visual arts, and philosophy. Pérez is also the author of a number of literary works, among them *The Divine Duty of Servants* (Cool Grove, 1999), *The Electric Comedy* (Cool Grove Press, 2000), and *The Lining of Our Souls: Excursions into Selected Paintings of Edward Hopper* (Cool Grove Press, 2002). His work has been athologized in *The Norton Anthology of Latino Literature* (2012). His most recent publication, *Severo Sarduy and the Neo-Baroque Image of Thought in the Visual Arts* was published in 2011 by Purdue University Press. 2016 saw the publication of two edited books of essays, *Agorapoetics: Poetics after Postmodernism*, and *Filosofía y culturas hispánicas: nuevas perspectivas,* co-edited with Nuria Morgado. And in 2017 *La comedia eléctrica*, a translation by Óscar Curieses of *The Electric Comedy* was published by Amargord Ediciones in Madrid.

www.ingramcontent.com/pod-product-compliance
Lightning Source LLC
Chambersburg PA
CBHW021131080526
44587CB00012B/1240